This book belongs to:

Made in United States
Orlando, FL
09 May 2024

46674152R00062